The Other Side Of ENDURANCE
Robert & Theresa Greene

THE WORKBOOK

Wherefore seeing we also are compassed about with so great a cloud of witnesses, let us lay aside every weight, and the sin which doth so easily beset us, and let us run with patience the race that is set before us. Looking unto Jesus the author and finisher of our faith; who for the joy that was set before him **endured** the cross, despising the shame, and is set down at the right hand of the throne of God.

Hebrews 12:1-2

Scripture quotations are taken from the *King James Version* of the *Holy Bible*.

<u>The Other Side Of Endurance: The Workbook</u> Copyright© 2008, by Robert and Theresa Greene

Adapted by Kim Bradford

Edited by Bertha Greene

Cover and Graphic Designs by Felicia Andrews

All rights reserved

No part of this book may be reproduced or transmitted in any form by any means without the written permission of the publisher.

ISBN 978-0-9748584-6-3

For more information, please write:
Covenant of Love Marriage Ministry, LLC
P. O. Box 78003
Greensboro, NC 27427-8109
Email: covoflove@gmail.com

Contents

Acknowledgments ii

Author's Message iii

Introduction 6

To Have and To Hold 8

For Better 14

For Worse 20

For Richer 27

For Poorer 32

In Sickness & In Health 39

Forsaking All Others 46

Until Death Do Us Part 52

Conclusion 59

Acknowledgments

Thank You Kim for allowing the Holy Spirit to ignite you to get this workbook done. "It was like fire shut up in your bones."

Thank You Bert for being ready to fulfill your commitment to edit the workbook and for the Lord managing your time.

Thank You Felicia for allowing the Lord to use you to help us get this workbook finished. You just took hold and got it done.

❧ *Authors' Message* ☙

To Couples

We pray that you have purchased and read our book, *The Other Side Of Endurance*, and that it was a blessing to you and yours. God is the keeper of our souls, and we should know it well.

We suggest that you complete the exercises in *The Workbook* separately to allow yourself the opportunity to be clear and honest with your answers, and then come together for the discussion, prayer and signing of the commitment statements.

Our desire is to *reveal* the obstacles we allowed to come into our lives, to *expose* the attacks of the enemy on marriage, and to *encourage* you to avoid repeating the same mistakes. Our prayer is that you will grow together and realize the power and value of shifting the focus in your marriage from your own personal course to a path of strength and enlightenment towards God.

Robert & Theresa Greene

Introduction

Marriage is a lifetime commitment and covenant. It should be entered into with much thought, prayer, preparation, and understanding of your needs and your future spouse's needs. Pre-marital counseling helps to uncover potential areas of conflict, and you should take advantage of this opportunity and insist that it be made available to you by your local church or Christian outreach organizations.

God created Eve for Adam, and if you have found the person who God created for you, you are blessed and highly favored. God knew that you and your spouse would be joined together long before your mom met your dad. Isn't it awesome to know that your marriage was predestined by God? He also knew that he would have to be in the center of your relationship in order for it to grow.

God has a perfect will for each of our lives, but he also has a perfect will for your marriage. He gave you gifts and abilities that you need to be successful in life, and those things that you lack he gave to your spouse so together you can do great things for his kingdom. God is truly worthy of your praise and glory for being the ultimate matchmaker.

In our book *The Other Side Of Endurance: A Marriage Ministry Birthed Through Perseverance*, there are numerous examples of how we are opposite of each other. Those differences during the early years of our marriage were a source of conflict, but now we realize that God purposely made us different so we can complement each other.

Introduction

If you are trying to make your spouse a carbon copy of you, stop it now. How can you grow if your spouse thinks, acts, and enjoys the exact same things you do? You grow when you are introduced to new things and new ideas, and you should celebrate your spouse for being different than you. Only God can change a person, and our goal is for God to begin his work in you.

Allowing God to affect change in every aspect of your life will not only bless your spouse, but it will bless you also. We hope our book and this companion workbook will encourage you that your latter days can be better than your former days. We wish we had these resources available to us in the early years of our marriage. Whether you are engaged or have been married a few years or many years, it is never too late or too early to work on your marriage so you can reap a bountiful harvest from your labor of love.

❡ Chapter 1 ❡

To Have and to Hold

Most men like this part of the marriage vows. It is pretty straightforward to them, and means that "this woman is mine, and I can have her and hold her for as much as I want and for as long as I want." Women like this marriage vow also since it probably means "my lonely days are over; this man is going to cuddle with me, and take care of me all the days of my life."

❡

What does *to have and to hold* mean to you?

_____
_____
_____
_____
_____

What do you think this phrase means to your spouse?

_____
_____
_____
_____
_____

Please review each other's answers and combine them to create a joint definition.

_____

_____

_____

_____

In Ephesians 5:25, the bible says the following about *to have and to hold:* "Husbands, love your wives, even as Christ also loved the church, and gave himself for it…"

Men have a great responsibility in taking a wife. In Ephesians, God's Word compares a man's love for his wife to that of Christ's love for the church. Christ loved unselfishly while giving instruction, protection, and ultimately, his life. Men should use Christ as an example for how to give and show love to their wives.

Like the church, the wife's response should be one of love, devotion, trust, and submission. Women, don't take for granted your husband's love for you. It should be cherished and nurtured; and most important, your love for your husband should be freely and unconditionally given.

As children, we get our first glimpse of marriage through our parents, other relatives, neighbors, and even our media driven culture. Unconsciously, we store this information, and it manifests itself in our marriage. When we bring negative preconceived notions into the marriage,

To Have and To Hold

or expectations that are not compatible with our spouse's desires and needs, then conflict, confusion, and unhappiness can begin to grow. How do we curb this friction? By looking in the mirror and consistently recognizing two individuals, not one. It is important for you to examine how your thoughts and actions affect your spouse.

Open communication is a great starting point to move your marriage in the right direction. Please complete the following sentences honestly, and then ask your spouse to share his/her responses with you. This is a chance for you to express your feelings and for your spouse to express his/her feelings. Each of you should listen and avoid your natural impulse or tendency to become defensive or accusatory.

సంఘ

1. I treat my spouse like a _____.
   a. disposable cup
   b. plastic cup
   c. drinking glass
   d. crystal flute

2. My spouse treats me like a _____.
   a. disposable cup
   b. plastic cup
   c. drinking glass
   d. crystal flute

3. I meet _____.
   a. all of my spouse's needs
   b. most of my spouse's needs
   c. some of my spouse's needs
   d. few of my spouse's needs
   e. none of my spouse's needs

4. My spouse meets _____.
   a. all of my needs
   b. most of my needs
   c. some of my needs
   d. few of my needs
   e. none of my needs

5. I desire _____ attention from my spouse.
   a. a lot more
   b. more
   c. a lot less
   d. less
   e. the current level of

6. My spouse desires _____ attention from me.
   a. a lot more
   b. more
   c. a lot less
   d. less
   e. the current level of

7. I desire _____ intimacy with my spouse.
   a. a lot more
   b. more
   c. a lot less
   d. less
   e. the current level of

8. My spouse desires _____ intimacy with me.
   a. a lot more
   b. more
   c. a lot less
   d. less
   e. the current level of

9. I would like to become a better _____ for my spouse.
   a. financial provider
   b. housekeeper
   c. friend
   d. lover
   e. communicator
   f. other _____

10. I would like for my spouse to become a better _____ to me.
    a. financial provider
    b. housekeeper
    c. friend
    d. lover
    e. communicator
    f. other _____

Were there any surprises? Did your answers show where you need improvement? Did your spouse uncover areas where she/he needs to improve? If so, identify two things that you will purposefully and prayerfully commit to improve.

TO HAVE AND TO HOLD COMMITMENT STATEMENT

I commit to improve _____ and
_____.

_____   _____
Signed by   Date

_____   _____
Witnessed and signed by spouse   Date

Please revisit this commitment statement with your spouse. Make sure you acknowledge and celebrate any positive changes that you see in your spouse based on his/her commitment statement, and don't be ashamed to ask for recognition for the progress you make toward change.

On _____, my spouse has fulfilled his/her commitment and promise.

_____   _____
Signed by   Date

_____   _____
Acknowledged and signed by spouse Date

To Have and To Hold

His closing prayer

Lord, I come to you thanking you for this woman that you created for me. Show me how to love her unselfishly unto death as Christ loved the church. Lord, help me to become a better partner to my wife and to provide her with all the things that she needs and desires from me. I ask you Lord to use me as a vessel that will protect, cherish, and cover her with love daily. I freely submit to you my body as a living sacrifice that can be used for your service and as an instrument to manifest your love for _____ *(insert wife's name)*. In Jesus' name, I pray. Amen.

Her closing prayer

Lord, I come to you thanking you for this man that you created for me to support and love. Show me how to submit to him as the church submits to Christ. Lord, help me to become a better partner to my husband and to provide him with all the things he needs and desires from me. I ask you Lord to use me as a vessel that will support, encourage, and reverence him with love daily. I freely submit to you my body as a living sacrifice that can be used for your service and as an instrument to manifest your love for _____ *(insert your husband's name)*. In Jesus' name, I pray. Amen.

❦ Chapter 2 ❧

For Better

> "***For Better***. This is the first vow of marital bliss. Newlyweds hope the honeymoon phase will never end. Everything is stimulating, warm and fresh as a 'bed of roses.' If ***'for better'*** were a permanent condition, there would be no such thing as marital tension, separation or divorce. Infidelity, irresponsibility, and insensitivity would be a thing of the past."
>
> The Other Side of Endurance
Introduction, p. 24

For better is the part of marriage that everyone longs for. Didn't you grow up believing in *for better* when you read fairy tales that always ended with the phrase "…and they lived happily ever after?" If so, you're not alone. Those fantasies will usually follow you to the altar, and in the forefront of your mind on your wedding day, the imagination runs wild with dreams of *for better*.

Most young couples make the mistake of spending so much time and energy on planning their wedding day that they neglect to plan for the lifetime commitment that marriage requires. It is so easy to overlook mishaps on the wedding day because everything is glossed over with the tint of rose colored glasses. The shades of reality take over when the fairy dust settles. In the course of the marriage, mishaps will occur and cause major tension and strife between spouses.

For Better

God wants the *for better* in your vows to be maintained throughout your marriage. The good times define *for better*, but the bad times refine it. An appreciation for warmth is more intense when you know the discomfort of feeling chilled. Similarly, the seasons of life will affect your marriage, and each season can deepen your love. Only after the cycle of a cold wintry experience can you find the promise of a fresh spring that will evolve into a sultry, hot summer before a rich, fruitful harvest ultimately emerges. Marriage follows the pattern of God's order for the universe. It is born, grows, stresses, pieces die, and new life replenishes what's lost with the proper balance of patience, nurturing, and healing over time. The result is a bond of strength in your relationship that could not have been built with only good times. Your marriage becomes solid from having been tested, tried and true. This is what we call *The Other Side Of Endurance*. How do you and your spouse get there together? The key is for you to recognize that the road to *for better* is an arduous, continuous process. Please do not short circuit the process because those cold, lonely days can lead to passion-filled nights. Afternoon arguments that leave you feeling chilly toward your spouse can be resolved in warmth, forgiveness, and a renewed sense of mutual appreciation and love.

⊰⊱

What season is your marriage in today?

__ Winter – cold and lonely   __ Summer – hot and steamy
__ Spring – renewed and rekindled   __ Fall – fruitful and frosty

What season do you want your marriage in today?

__ Winter – cold and lonely   __ Summer – hot and steamy
__ Spring – renewed and rekindled   __ Fall – fruitful and frosty

For Better

If the current season of your marriage is in conflict with the season you desire, then there is work for you to do. Perhaps you and your spouse have different love languages. Some people are stimulated visually by their spouse's facial features and/or body shape. Others may be stimulated audibly by words that are spoken and/or the tone, while others may be stimulated by their spouse's touch, which includes caressing, hugging, and kissing.

Which love language do you prefer?	Which love language does your spouse prefer?
Visual ☐	Visual ☐
Audible ☐	Audible ☐
Touch ☐	Touch ☐
Other: _____	Other: _____

Many spouses do not share the same love language. If this is the case in your marriage, then you must learn to compromise. If your love language is audible, and your spouse prefers to touch, then sometimes you may have to cuddle, and seek nothing from your spouse in return. It is important to be patient with your spouse during this time. After unselfishly focusing on your spouse, his or her mood should improve. It is then appropriate for you to reassure your mate that you will continue showing physical affection for his/her pleasure, and balance the conversation by expressing your own personal sense of fulfillment, appreciation and desire to hear "I love you" more often.

Let thy fountain be blessed: and rejoice with the wife of thy youth (Proverbs 5:18). This passage of scripture reveals to us that marriage is blessed by God. It also lets us know that it is designed to be joyous and filled with cheer. When you look at your spouse, do you reflect back on the butterflies in your stomach or the excitement you felt when you were pronounced man and wife? Those emotions can be stirred up again, and what you felt on your wedding day is only the tip of the iceberg of the *for better* moments that God wants you to enjoy during your marriage.

For Better

FOR BETTER COMMITMENT STATEMENT ❧

I commit to do _____ and

_____

_____ so that my marriage will be the source of joy that God intended for my spouse and me to enjoy.

_____   _____
Signed by   Date

_____   _____
Witnessed and signed by spouse   Date

Don't forget to document the day that this commitment pledge was fulfilled to your spouse's satisfaction.

On _____, my spouse has fulfilled his/her commitment and promise.

_____   _____
Signed by   Date

_____   _____
Acknowledged and signed by spouse   Date

His closing prayer

Lord, I ask you to show me how to express love to _____ (insert wife's name) in a manner that is pleasing to you so that I can experience *for better* with her. Like Paul, please Lord, help me to be content in all things, even the trying seasons that our marriage goes through. Lead me. Guide me. And, order my footsteps so I will not lead her down a path that will cause hurt or harm. Please reveal to me areas where I am weak as a husband and help me to improve. Thank you for the gift of marriage and my wife with whom I share my life. In Jesus' name, I pray. Amen.

Her closing prayer

Lord, I ask you to show me how to express love to _____ (insert husband's name) in a manner that is pleasing to you so that I can experience *for better* with him. Like Paul, please Lord, help me to be content in all things, even the trying seasons that our marriage goes through. Teach me how to support and encourage him in my deeds and let the words of my mouth cause him no hurt or harm. Please reveal to me areas where I am weak as a wife, and please, Lord God, help me to improve. Thank you for the gift of marriage and my husband with whom I share my life. In Jesus' name, I pray. Amen.

☙ Chapter 3 ❧

For Worse

In marriage, as in life, there will be unhappy days that can be caused by unplanned pregnancies, mounting debt, unrealistic expectations, abuse, and infidelity. How you respond to these issues will define your marriage. These issues will strengthen, weaken or destroy your marriage. But, remember this: the success or failure of your marriage depends on the choices you make and the actions you take when tough times challenge the bond of your vows, because that bond embodies your commitment to God and to one another.

All marriages encounter difficulty. In previous chapters, we learned that marriage was created and blessed by God, which means it is hated by the enemy, whose mission is to steal, kill, and destroy everything aligned with God's plan for your life. Christians are challenged even more, and our faith leads us to Christ as an anchor when the tempest rages and the pillars of matrimony are blown off course. We always have a choice. Will you choose to walk in faith as Jesus commands through the storms of marriage? Or… will you choose to focus on yourself in the storm and allow your marriage to die in the midst of your turmoil? When sunshine beams through a rain storm, a beautiful rainbow appears in the sky to indicate the worst is over, and the promise of a brighter day ahead. The same is true when you allow the promise of God's strength and love to shine through the turbulence of a marital storm. Storms by nature will cease. The survival of your marriage is determined by the position you take and the choices you make during the storm.

For Worse

Our life's experience revealed in *The Other Side Of Endurance* and this workbook is a testimony to the fact that God's radiance will shine through the most threatening clouds following the storm and show you something beautiful! We have never been happier in our marriage. But, *'don't get it twisted'...* the test and trials along the way were at times gut wrenching and nearly back breaking. When we thought we were at our wits' end, with the marriage hanging on by a thread at the very end of our rope, **God** was our lifeline. Praise Jesus! So, then, we are witnesses that if he is able to deliver and keep us together through all that we have endured, he can do the same for you. Nothing is too great for God. Take yourself out of the equation and give it to God. Then, and only then, will *for worse* be turned around.

Which trait(s) best reflects your reaction during marital conflicts.	How does your spouse normally handle conflict?
Yell/Argue	Yell/Argue
Avoid	Avoid
Push/Hit	Push/Hit
Silent treatment	Silent treatment
Discuss	Discuss
Apologize	Apologize
Turn to a friend	Turn to a friend
Cry	Cry

For Worse

If you answered that you push and/or hit your spouse during conflicts, seek anger management counseling as soon as possible. It is NEVER acceptable to physically abuse your spouse.

If you answered that you avoid conflict by giving your mate the silent treatment, you are communicating, but not effectively. This can lead to distance in your marriage. Conflict is normal. Avoiding it and choosing not to verbally address your issues will lead to greater problems later because unresolved conflict always resurfaces.

If you answered that you yell, argue, or cry, an emotional balance is needed in your response to conflict. When you consistently respond to conflict by letting your emotions soar with crying or yelling, you hinder effective communications because you are too upset to properly convey your own issues or hear what your spouse is saying to you. More than likely, the conflict will not be resolved when you can not remain calm enough to discuss issues rationally.

If you answered that you turn to a friend when conflict arises, beware. This can lead to more trouble. This is especially true if your friend is of the opposite sex. You are developing an unhealthy attachment to this person, and this should be nipped in the bud and brought to an end, especially if your spouse is not a part of the friendship. If your friend is of the same sex, this can be equally as disruptive to the marriage. It is critically important that the person you turn to remains impartial and is capable to provide you with godly counsel.

For Worse

Discussing and talking through conflict with your spouse is the best response. Disagreements are normal, and one of the greatest challenges in marriage is to communicate your point of view without losing control of yourself, which includes control of your emotions. After you have expressed your point of view, it is critical for you to listen to your spouse's point of view, and then together, reasonably come to terms to resolve the matter.

Dealing effectively with conflict in the *for worse* times is one of the best skills you can acquire and possess in marriage. During those *for worse* times, watch, pray, and pay close attention to how you spend your time as a couple. Things will begin to improve when you release the urge to handle things on your own terms and prayerfully turn to the Lord and one another for strength through your situation.

ಜಂಗ

Choose all that apply to you and your spouse. During difficult times, we:
__ Pray together
__ Go to church
__ Seek wisdom from godly friends
__ Fast
__ Talk with pastor or someone in church leadership
__ Read the bible

All the above are positive actions to engage in together during difficult times. The more answers you chose, the more likely you and your mate will be able to persevere through difficult times. If you only chose a few

For Worse

responses, and you are struggling to get through the challenges that difficult days bring, then we encourage you to incorporate more of the choices above into your marriage when it is shaken with trouble.
You have probably already noticed that each chapter in this workbook ends with a prayer. We have designed it that way because we want you to know that asking the Lord to stabilize your marriage will turn things around. And, this is especially true when your marriage is staring periods of *for worse* dead in the face.

John 15:12 says *This is my commandment, That ye love one another, as I have loved you.* What does this mean? It means that you are to follow the example of Jesus who always forgives and offers love no matter how great or small the offense whenever we make mistakes and ask for forgiveness. Showering your spouse with unconditional love and forgiveness will greatly reduce your *for worse* days. If your spouse is unsaved, then this may be a more difficult task for you, but God can use you to initiate divine change in your spouse and your marriage.

FOR WORSE COMMITMENT STATEMENT

I commit to do _____

and _____

so that the *for worse* days will not weaken or destroy my marriage.

_____ _____
Signed by   Date

_____ _____
Witnessed and signed by spouse   Date

Don't forget to document the day that this commitment pledge was fulfilled to your spouse's satisfaction.

On _____, my spouse has fulfilled his/her commitment and promise.

_____ _____
Signed by   Date

_____ _____
Acknowledged and signed by spouse Date

For Worse

His closing prayer

Lord, I thank you for my marriage and the good days as well as the bad that we have experienced. My desire is to love and forgive _____ *(insert wife's name)* more freely in times of trouble just as you love and forgive me when I fall short in pleasing you. Lord, help me to learn the lessons that can only be taught through trials and tribulations, and may these experiences grow us closer to you and to each other. In the name of Jesus, I stand against any and all attacks that the enemy will use to destroy my marriage. I will continue to seek your face in times of trouble, and I will not faint or get weary in well doing. In Jesus' name, I pray. Amen.

Her closing prayer

Lord, I thank you for my marriage and the good days as well as the bad that we have experienced. My desire is to love and forgive _____ *(insert husband's name)* more freely in times of trouble just as you love and forgive me when I fall short in pleasing you. Lord, help me to learn the lessons that can only be taught through trials and tribulations, and may these experiences grow us closer to you and to each other. In the name of Jesus, I stand against any and all attacks that the enemy will use to destroy my marriage. I will continue to seek your face in times of trouble, and I will not faint or get weary in well doing. In Jesus' name, I pray. Amen.

Chapter 4

For Richer

This is another portion of the marriage vows that comes easy for many people. It is easy to pledge your love to another in times of prosperity, especially if your mate is generous and makes wise decisions in the times of plenty. To many women, times of prosperity equal security. To many men, times of prosperity equal confidence and reassurance that he is a good provider. Let's examine your roles in helping to keep your marriage in good financial standing.

On a scale from 1 to 10, with 1 being the lowest, and 10 being the highest, how would you rate yourself in each of the following scenarios? When you have finished, be prepared to discuss your responses with your spouse to see if he/she agrees.

1. I like to save money. 1 2 3 4 5 6 7 8 9 10
2. I like to spend money. 1 2 3 4 5 6 7 8 9 10
3. I like to invest money. 1 2 3 4 5 6 7 8 9 10
4. I like to pay bills on time. 1 2 3 4 5 6 7 8 9 10
5. I regularly borrow money from family and friends. 1 2 3 4 5 6 7 8 9 10
6. I feel stressed when the bank account is low. 1 2 3 4 5 6 7 8 9 10
7. I feel happy when the bank account is high. 1 2 3 4 5 6 7 8 9 10
8. I think I should contribute more financially to the household. 1 2 3 4 5 6 7 8 9 10
9. I share my views about finances with my spouse. 1 2 3 4 5 6 7 8 9 10
10. I value money highly. 1 2 3 4 5 6 7 8 9 10

Did you and your spouse agree or disagree on your responses? If there is a big difference in your ratings, for example, if you gave yourself a 10, and your spouse thought you deserved a 1, then record those differences.

_____

_____

_____

_____

_____

_____

These issues need to be addressed. Discuss the rationale of your own ratings, and ask your spouse to do the same. Give specific and numerous examples in your explanation. This discussion will typically reveal one truth—the person who provides the most recent examples to support his/her ratings is probably the person whose score is most accurate. Do your best to discuss and understand each other's ratings and to reach a compromise on the score. If you are unable to mutually agree on your ratings in each scenario, then revise your score to reflect the numbered rating of the person who is able to provide the most accurate, recent examples to support his/her score.

If your scores matched, use the space above to note those areas where you and your spouse view money similarly or differently. For example, if you and your spouse both recognize that you are not a saver, but your spouse is a saver, then document that. This will help to give both of you a clearer picture on which spouse is fiscally more responsible. As a couple, you will benefit greatly as you find a way to capitalize on this strength to improve and/or maintain your financial health.

For Richer

Does *for richer* have to always equate with money? *For where your treasure is, there will your heart be also* (Matthew 6:21). Can you name 3 things you value more than money?

1. _____

2. _____

3. _____

Please share and compare these responses with your spouse. Do you see similarities? Do you see differences? These answers reveal your values. If you find that you and your mate value different things, then you need to discuss these differences and find a compromise that you both can agree on.

For Richer

FOR RICHER COMMITMENT STATEMENT ∞

I commit to do _____

and _____

so that the *for richer* days will be long lasting throughout my marriage.

_____   _____
Signed by   Date

_____   _____
Witnessed and signed by spouse   Date

Don't forget to document the day that this commitment pledge was fulfilled to your spouse's satisfaction.

On _____, my spouse has fulfilled his/her commitment and promise.

_____   _____
Signed by   Date

_____   _____
Acknowledged and signed by spouse Date

His closing prayer

Lord, I know you are a God of more than enough. Thank you for the riches you have bestowed upon our marriage. I ask that you help me to be a better steward over that which you bless me to provide for my family. I know that prosperity to you means that nothing is lacking, so I ask you to prosper _____ *(insert wife's name)* in all of her ways, and that I do nothing to detract from all the blessings that you have in store for her. Thank you for _____ *(insert wife's name)* because she is one of the greatest blessings that you have ever given to me. In Jesus' name, I pray. Amen.

Her closing prayer

Lord, I know you are a God of more than enough. Thank you for the riches you have bestowed upon our marriage. I ask that you help me to be a better steward over that which you've blessed our family to have. I know that prosperity to you means that nothing is lacking, and I ask you to prosper _____ *(insert husband's name)* in all of his ways, and that I do nothing to detract from all the blessings that you have in store for him. Thank you for _____ *(insert husband's name)* because he is one of the greatest blessings that you have ever given to me. In Jesus' name, I pray. Amen.

⋈ Chapter 5 ⋈

For Poorer

"I can do bad all by myself." Does this phrase sound familiar? I have heard men and women say this phrase when the money gets funny. The reality is many people can deal with times of lack when they are by themselves, but when they marry, somehow those bad times are compounded when one partner inevitably blames the other for most of the financial woes. What do you think about this? Is it ever justifiable? Do you think it would be easier for you to take your eyes off what you have done to contribute to your financial difficulties and look directly at your husband/wife as the sole source of blame? The fact is the blame game never has a winner. Regardless of fault, you're in the marriage as a team, and your mission together should be to build or rebuild a solid financial foundation so the misery of *for poorer* becomes a condition of the past.

Now, holding things down when money is short is a major challenge. Financial difficulties are one of the leading causes of divorce. Low wages, mounting debt, bad credit, high interest credit cards, unemployment, etc., can damage a man's pride because most men believe the role and responsibility of the man is to provide for his family. His mood will probably not be the best during these times, so if you are a woman who constantly complains during this period, please realize that you are making the situation worse. On the other hand, husbands, it is natural for your wife's stress level to increase when there is not enough money to pay bills and meet basic needs, especially when children are involved. When you ignore her anxiety or belittle her for experiencing these emotions, you are not helping the situation either.

Couples must work together in times of difficulty. If you have ever watched any team play a sport successfully, then you have observed individual players who work well with others to achieve a goal. The team's priority is to win, and each player works as hard as necessary in sync with other team members and leaders to get the victory. The same is true of marriage. Knowing the leaders and strongest team members of your team is important. In a Christian marriage, Christ is the owner, CEO, and head coach. When you acknowledge and follow the leadership of Jesus, you will have a vision of hope and faith for future prosperity, even during times of lack. In the midst of financial instability, mental and spiritual stability can be maintained by your dependence on God's Word. In Galatians 5:22-23, you will find listed the fruit of the Spirit. Focusing on God, the ability to overcome **anything** is possible with love, joy, peace, longsuffering, gentleness, goodness, faith, meekness, and temperance. Another word for longsuffering is patience. When money is tight, patience is the key to understanding that your condition did not happen overnight, and will not be solved overnight. Given time, patience, and diligence, the Lord will give you wisdom to get out of your dire financial situation. Meekness and temperance are also known as gentleness and self-control. A kind word goes a long way when times are tough. Saying something kind when you want to say something condescending or self righteous takes self control! Sit back husbands, and watch your wife's response to your words of reassurance coupled with positive actions. Wives, you might want to fight the urge to show resentment and try a softer approach

For Poorer

too. Sit back and watch your husband's response to your words of encouragement coupled with actions of support. Your active, conscious demonstrations of the fruit of the Spirit during the roughest times in your marriage will yield a renewed commitment from your spouse to work with you to solve your problems and his/her attitude will improve.

Proverbs 3:5-6 reads *Trust in the Lord with all thine heart; and lean not unto thine own understanding. In all thy ways acknowledge him, and he shall direct thy paths.* The marital path is filled with twists and turns. Sometimes, navigating the turns together will bring immediate blessings; other times, it will lead to trouble. What counts most is that you stay on course to reach the goal line of every path together.

In times of financial lack, how do you and your spouse react? Pick three or more character traits that describe your own reaction in times of financial difficulty.

Panic	Denial	Defensive
Angry	Indifferent	Defeated
Worried	Problem solver	Prayer warrior
Depressed	Burden bearer	Optimistic
Frustrated	Resentful	Avoidance
Pessimistic	Overwhelmed	Blamer
Dismissive	Resourceful	Violent

For Poorer 35

Pick three or more character traits that describe the reaction of your spouse in times of financial difficulty.

Panic	Denial	Defensive
Angry	Indifferent	Defeated
Worried	Problem solver	Prayer warrior
Depressed	Burden bearer	Optimistic
Frustrated	Resentful	Avoidance
Pessimistic	Overwhelmed	Blamer
Dismissive	Resourceful	Violent

Compare your responses to those of your spouse. Are they similar? Discuss your differences. If any of the character traits your spouse exhibits make the situation worse, share what you think can be done differently to improve your situation. In addition, get feedback from your spouse on what you can do differently during times best described by *for poorer*.

Earlier in this chapter, you studied a simple yet important step you can take to shorten the season of *for poorer*. As a couple, decide which spouse is better with managing money. Gender should play no role in your decision. A man who is the head of his home should be secure enough to 'man up,' recognize his limitations, and delegate tasks to his wife for the health of the household. Likewise, a submissive wife will trust her husband if he decides he is better at managing the family finances.

For Poorer

Even when you are financially broken, remember to pay your tithes because God will bless you if you are obedient to his Word. A good plan is to pay God first, and then yourself. No matter how tight funds are, you will eventually prosper if you consistently set aside funds to put into a savings account and/or retirement plan, e.g., IRA, CD, or mutual fund. The internet is a valuable resource of information about how to minimize debt. Alternatively, you might consider seeking the professional advice of a reputable credit counselor to reduce or eliminate your debt.

HIS FOR POORER COMMITMENT STATEMENT ❧

I commit to do _____

and _____

so the *for poorer* days will be brief throughout my marriage.

_____   _____

Signed by   Date

_____   _____

Witnessed and signed by spouse   Date

Don't forget to document the day that this commitment pledge was fulfilled to your spouse's satisfaction.

On _____, my spouse has fulfilled his/her commitment and promise.

_____   _____

Signed by   Date

_____   _____

Acknowledged and signed by spouse   Date

For Poorer

His & Her closing prayer
(Recite together)

Lord, we know you are a God who answers prayers. Thank you for being an ever present help in the time of trouble. Thank you for directing our path even now to look to you to help us get out of this financial bondage. We know that the enemy comes to steal, kill, and destroy, but you have come to give us life more abundantly. Please watch over us and give us the wisdom to turn this situation around together. Have your way in our marriage and home, and let your will be done. We know the enemy meant this situation for evil, and you can turn it around to be used for our good. We love you and honor you. In Jesus' name, we pray. Amen.

Chapter 6

In Sickness & In Health

One of the first lessons in the bible teaches us about the shame Adam and Eve experienced when they discovered their nakedness in the Garden of Eden after disobeying God. Adam and Eve's confusion was a result of being out of the will of God. Marriage is ordained by God, so when you and your spouse unite in holy matrimony, you are physically and spiritually connected and covered as you walk in God's will. One of the many beauties of marriage is knowing that God has blessed you with a mate who accepts you for you. In your marriage, there should be 'no shame in your game' or unwillingness to expose your body or physical condition in the presence of your spouse. Your marriage will be blessed as you become transparent with your spouse, and the love only grows stronger when 'you' are willing to share and expose *all* of 'you' — the good, the bad, and the ugly.

As sure as day turns to night, the time will come when you physically feel less than one hundred percent. In times of sickness, learn to share your pain, and lean on your mate. Do not rob your spouse of the opportunity to be there for you. When you need help, consider yourself blessed to have someone near you who sees beyond the surface and offers to help you. No matter how independent you are under normal circumstances, *in sickness,* you would do well for yourself and the marriage to relax, expose your vulnerabilities, and graciously accept the assistance of your wife/husband. Needing help from your spouse does not make you weak, dependent, or burdensome; it makes you human. In Chapter 3, we covered the

In Sickness and In Health

importance of talking to your spouse about issues of concern rather than turning to a friend outside the marriage. A similar principle applies during seasons of illness. The wedding vow *in sickness and in health* means that you have a committed partner by your side in the best and worst physical states, and accordingly, you should turn to your spouse before anyone else, including your mother, father, sister, brother, child, or friend. *In sickness and in health* is a vow that should not be uttered or taken lightly. It is important to support your spouse by providing the love and care required no matter what physical condition you are challenged to deal with. Patience, respect, and kindness are key during periods of illness. If you are the person receiving care, always remember to express gratitude and appreciation for the love and attention given by your spouse. No one wants to feel used or unappreciated.

☙❧

Below are several statements. Please mark each one either true or false. After you have completed the exercise, share and compare your answers with your spouse and discuss why you think your response best describes how you react in seasons of sickness and whether or not you should work together to improve in any of these areas.

1. When I am sick, I feel comfortable talking to my spouse about how my body feels and do my best to describe my condition.

    TRUE _____   FALSE _____

2. When my spouse is sick, he/she feels comfortable talking to me about how his/her body feels and does his/her best to describe the condition.

    TRUE _____   FALSE _____

In Sickness and In Health

3. When I am sick, I turn to my spouse for support before I lean heavily on friends and family.

   TRUE _____   FALSE _____

4. When my spouse is sick, he/she turns to me for support before leaning heavily on friends and family.

   TRUE _____   FALSE _____

5. When I am sick, I let my spouse know how much I appreciate his/her help.

   TRUE _____   FALSE _____

6. When my spouse is sick, he/she lets me know how much my help is appreciated.

   TRUE _____   FALSE _____

ಸಂಐ

If neither you nor your spouse has experienced illness during your marriage, then you should be very thankful to God because good health is nothing to be taken for granted. You are in a very enviable position and are blessed beyond measure. Continue to do the things that contribute to the fitness of your body. Exercise, proper diet, drinking plenty of water, and nutritional supplements, help to keep your body strong. Being wise about your health today can pay dividends in the future. As your age increases, so does the likelihood that you or your spouse will experience illness.

Since the timing of most illnesses is unpredictable, planning for medical setbacks is nearly impossible. Unplanned sickness can put a strain on marriage. An injury at work that results in lost wages, a car accident that leaves a healthy person with a permanent disability, cancer that develops without warning, or a child born with a birth defect can take a toll on the individual patient, as well as the family. The stress and heartache of a sudden serious illness can test the strength of your character, fidelity, and commitment to your spouse and your marriage.

How can you be prepared to cope? Be prayerful always, especially in difficult times. God specifically made you for your situation. This is not the time to become angry with God or your spouse, or to become depressed, hopeless, withdrawn, or bitter. It rains on the just as well as the unjust, and you may be challenged to accept the fact that life is not fair according to your own standards. While bad things can and do happen to good people, you have an upper hand when you trust in God and hold on to your faith. Remember Jeremiah 29:11. *For I know the thoughts that I think toward you, saith the Lord, thoughts of peace, and not of evil, to give you an expected end.* This is a powerful scripture to meditate and stand on when you feel life has dealt you a tough hand or an unfair blow.

If you know anything about boxing, each boxer is trained to take a hit and deliver a hit. So too are you trained by God! In Romans 8:37, the bible says *in all these things we are more than conquerors through him that loved us*. This means that you are equipped by God to handle anything this world throws at you. If you have faith to believe God's Word, then overcoming victory is already yours. When your body is broken, you and your spouse can have hope when your spirit remains whole! If your mind plays tricks on you, you can regain control in prayer by asking the Lord to fix it. Christian believers have a healer of the body, mind and soul. Why should you reject that Jesus paid it all on Calvary, and with his stripes you are healed? Exactly! You should never reject that truth. If you don't see it, claim it anyway and walk in faith until healing is manifested or until the Lord raises you to a level where his grace is sufficient for you to accept your situation and live peacefully with your condition.

Sometimes the Lord delays his response to see how you will react, and sometimes he allows you to go through difficulties in order to bless someone else. Trust God's will and worship and honor him while you are going through your medical crisis. Most people can praise God when everything is going well and their prayers are quickly answered. The true worshiper praises regardless, knowing that God dwells in the midst of praise. So, strive to be a worshiper. If your spouse is unsaved, it is critical that you stand in the gap for him/her and not be moved by what you see or what he/she says. This is when your faith will be tested. Avoid preachy self righteousness or words of condemnation with unbelievers. Choose a loving approach instead. Lean on God to lead you with a quiet strength so that every thought and deed for your ailing spouse serves to encourage, bless and pave the way to healing and salvation.

IN SICKNESS & IN HEALTH COMMITMENT STATEMENT ∞

I commit to do _____

and _____

so that my marriage will stay strong *in sickness and in health*.

.

_____   _____
Signed by   Date

_____   _____
Witnessed and signed by spouse   Date

Don't forget to document the day that this commitment pledge was fulfilled to your spouse's satisfaction.

On _____, my spouse has fulfilled his/her commitment and promise.

_____   _____
Signed by   Date

_____   _____
Acknowledged and signed by spouse   Date

His & Her closing prayer ≈
(Recite together)

Lord, use us to help others who need a word of encouragement. Show us individuals and couples with whom we can share our trials so we can learn more and grow from our journeys and struggles. Help us to know that trials come to perfect our faith, and that you put no more on us than we can bear. Help us to become transparent with each other so we can find safety and love in our marriage in the midst of a dying and unkind world. Thank you for the measure of health and faith you have given us, and we present our bodies as a living sacrifice to be used by you. In Jesus' name, we pray. Amen.

❦ Chapter 7 ❧
Forsaking All Others

On your wedding day, if you were anything like me, you saw your mate as the perfect choice for you, and the excitement of spending the rest of your life together sparked enough passion and hope, that you found it easy to embrace the wedding vow, *forsaking all others*. After all, the beauty of the relationship is respecting and cherishing your spouse above all others, so it's just 'icing on the cake' to seal and declare your mutual commitment to one another before God and every witness present at the wedding.

Fast forward a couple months. Day-to-day reality sets in, and you begin to question what you've gotten yourself into as you observe that your mate is messy, moody, and just plain gets on your nerves. Although you were spinning with ideas of perfection at the altar, you soon realize that your mate is incapable of meeting all your needs. You might feel cheated, disappointed, or generally disoriented about the marriage. Relax. Your thoughts and feelings are quite typical. Your challenge will be to develop more realistic expectations of your spouse, yourself, and the marriage to neutralize the negativity.

Please choose the answer that most closely reflects your thoughts.
SA=Strongly Agree, A=Agree, N=Neither Agree nor Disagree, SD=Strongly Disagree, D=Disagree

1. My spouse should meet most of my emotional needs. SA A N SD D
2. My spouse should meet most of my sexual needs. SA A N SD D
3. My spouse should meet most of my financial needs. SA A N SD D
4. My spouse should put my happiness over his/her own. SA A N SD D
5. My spouse should strive to please me. SA A N SD D

After you have completed your answers, please discuss them with your spouse. Explain your rationale for answering the questions as you did. Discuss how well you feel your spouse is or is not meeting your needs, and ask your spouse what he/she feels is his/her role in meeting your needs. So no one is left feeling frustrated and unloved, the final and most critical part of the exercise is for both of you to work together to develop realistic expectations for your spouse, yourself, and the marriage.

Learning to adjust expectations in the marriage serves to create a warm, peaceful, and loving home environment. Unrealistic expectations cause tension that can drive an emotional and physical wedge between partners. The result is escapism. Your spouse may begin to spend more time outside the home with a friend, or friends, to escape the pressure and vent about your marital problems. Again, this is a slippery slope. In Chapters 3 and 6, we studied the importance of handling stresses within the marriage. Turning to others outside the marriage, especially those of the opposite sex, can lead to trouble. This is what *"forsaking all others"* is all about— protecting the sanctity of your marriage by keeping your commitment of trust with God and your spouse. Everyone needs friends; however, you should be cautious about building friendships that help you evade your marital problems. These relationships are unhealthy because they will hinder the growth of your marriage. Such friendships need to be checked, altered, or terminated.

Ask your spouse to identify any friends who are hindering your marriage, and why those friends are being called out? You should also take this opportunity to identify friends of your spouse who you feel are hindering your marriage, and explain why you feel that way. Together, you should decide which friendships you will change, and which you will cut off in an effort to improve your marriage.

The hardest person for you to forsake is yourself. Do you see yourself as God sees you? Despite your imperfections, He still loves you and remains patient with you. Doesn't your spouse deserve the same treatment? Instead of focusing on his or her shortcomings, why not focus on the good, just as God does? When you begin to forsake yourself, you will be less likely to keep score on the number of times your spouse angers you, and you'll be less inclined to hold your spouse to an unrealistic standard. After adjusting your expectations with your mate, you will learn to treat your spouse as you would like to be treated without looking for anything in return. This unselfish demonstration of affection is exactly how God loves us. And, this is how we should learn to love one another. Be patient with your progress as you work toward this goal. It's a process.

Never lose sight of the fact that we are human, not divine. None of us is perfect. Sometimes, when we least expect to step to the left, we find ourselves caught up in situations that test our resolve as it relates to *forsaking all others*. Marriage doesn't translate into 'blindness' or 'isolation.' In the normal course of living, we will encounter others who are attractive and tempting. This is natural. This is also where your maturity and discipline will be tested. Be prudent. You wouldn't stick your head in the lion's den without expecting to sustain serious injury. If you are feeling neglected or disappointed in your marriage, there is sometimes a tendency to seek attention from a co-worker, or that person with the pretty smile, or some nameless person in a club. How much harm could result from the lonely spouse who seeks a little outside stimulation from an exotic dancer, an internet site, a text message, a 900 number, or a sex video? Immeasurable harm can result. Steer clear of the obvious pitfalls that can damage or destroy your marriage. When you seek your own solutions and leave God and your spouse out of the equation, your marriage will suffer. In the end, it does not matter whether you are the aggressor, the seducer, or the seduced. Somebody is bound to be the victim. *Forsaking all others* is more than lip service. It's love in action. It's discipline. It's forgiveness. It's praying and staying when you want to curse and run. It's **knowing** that God's grace is sufficient to keep you and your spouse united until you make it to *The Other Side Of Endurance*. And even then, every day will present a new challenge for you to kill the flesh and the selfish urges that arise. Marriage involves a life long commitment to each other, and we will study more about the longevity aspect of the institution in the next chapter.

Brethren, I count not myself to have apprehended: but this one thing I do, forgetting those things which are behind, and reaching forth unto those things which are before, I press toward the mark for the prize of the high calling of God in Christ Jesus. (Philippians 3:13-14) In this scripture, Paul was not specifically talking about marriage; however, the principle message in this text is key to its success. In marriage, one of the most valuable components is the process of forgiveness. It is important to forget your past mistakes and forgive yourself for them, and then it is equally as important to forget and forgive your spouse's past mistakes. This process of forgiveness is ongoing because everyone makes mistakes. Once you faithfully engage in this process, God can take your marriage to a higher level because forgiveness moves your marriage in the right direction, which is pleasing to Him.

FORSAKING ALL OTHERS COMMITMENT STATEMENT ◊

I commit to do _____

and _____

to reinforce my desire to improve my marriage and fulfill the wedding vow *forsaking all others*.

_____   _____
Signed by   Date

_____   _____
Witnessed and signed by spouse   Date

Don't forget to document the day that this commitment pledge was fulfilled to your spouse's satisfaction.

On _____, my spouse has fulfilled his/her commitment and promise.

_____   _____
Signed by   Date

_____   _____
Acknowledged and signed by spouse   Date

His & Her closing prayer

(Recite together)

Lord, we love, honor, and praise you for all the blessings you have bestowed upon us. Lord, help us not to have unrealistic expectations of each other. We will continue to look to you and follow you in good times and bad. We ask your guidance by revealing to us any people or thoughts that need to be forsaken in order to move our marriage to the next level. We will continuously forget and forgive each other for past hurts, and press toward the mark that you have set for us. We thank you for keeping us together, and we pray that our love for you and each other will continue to grow unconditionally. In Jesus' name, we pray. Amen.

❦ Chapter 8 ❧

<u>Until Death Do Us Part</u>

The vow *until death do us part* is the ultimate promise of fidelity, forgiveness and love. What separates the long lasting marriages from those that end in divorce court? Lack of trouble? Family pressures? Financial stress? Health and fitness? No. All marriages are tried and tested by these and other issues. The separating factor is total commitment to God and spouse even when it means reducing yourself, your pride, and your will so that God will get the glory in your marriage. As we examine this last wedding vow, please take a moment to consider all you have gained by studying about the realities of marriage. Now, flip back to the very first sentence in the Introduction of this workbook, and read it aloud. You might expect a book on marriage to begin with such a statement – simple, yet powerful. Now, read the statement again silently to fill your spirit with this fundamental truth about God's will for developing your relationship with your spouse. Yes. As you grow and develop individually throughout your life, each day also brings new experiences that mold your understanding and interaction with your husband or wife. The learning process is timeless. "Marriage is a lifetime commitment and covenant."

Of all the marriage vows, *"until death do us part"* sums up the 'God factor' that makes the difference. God is eternal. He always was, is, and will always be. In Revelation 22:13, the Lord says "I am Alpha and Omega, the beginning and the end, the first and the last." Leaning on the infinite wisdom and presence of God is the foundation for getting to *The Other Side Of Endurance*.

Until Death Do Us Part

Hopefully, you have already read our book. If so, then you know the crazy twists and turns our marriage took in its earlier years. We didn't even know and trust God as we know and trust him today, but we had godly people in our lives interceding on our behalf, i.e., praying for us when we were engaged in all kinds of foolishness that would have torn us apart as a couple and a family. It was nothing short of God's grace that kept us together through it all. It's in the book! Drama! Deceit! Financial Burdens! Babies! Broken Vows! These are often factors which precede decrees for divorce.

The most compelling reason we can give you for our victory is the 'God factor.' The marriage had taken a nose dive! And, the day we stopped giving all the energy to "I feel this… and I can't believe you would do that… and I'm not going to take it anymore…," i.e., the moment we began to humble ourselves, swallow the pride, read God's Word and practice what pleases the Lord despite our circumstances, the healing of the marriage began to manifest itself. Praise Jesus! We went through so many critical near misses and breaking points. Sometimes, it made no common sense that we even stuck it out.

At the time, we did not even realize that God was working it out so there would be such a time as this. God knew when we were 'wild, wooly, and completely out of hand,' that our marriage was a work in progress for our making, and more important, for the making and perfection of this testimony to the glory of God! In every crisis, God kept our hemorrhaging marriage intact through it all. We can stand firmly and declare that no

Until Death Do Us Part

problem is so great that it's insurmountable. God delivered our marriage from chaos to utopia. So, the purpose of our ministry is to give God praise for saving us, and to share the hard realities of our experience so you will be encouraged. If our marriage could survive all that we endured, then we believe you should know the 'God factor' can keep you too. So, speak boldly to God, your spouse, and yourself, and reaffirm your commitment of *until death do us part!*

In the space provided below, list several things that you would either like to rekindle or experience for the first time with your husband or wife in your lifetime together:

1. _____
2. _____
3. _____
4. _____
5. _____
6. _____
7. _____

Now, share your responses with your spouse, and note the similarities and differences in how you envision an infusion of quality into the future of your marriage. Do any of the answers come as a surprise? Consider and discuss what each of you thinks it will take, individually and collectively, to rekindle and/or realize some of the experiences you have listed above.

Your latter years can be much sweeter than your former years. Your marriage is a labor of love requiring prayer, communication, forgiveness, and endurance. With all you have learned here, you now have the knowledge and the tools, to succeed.

Having someone with whom to share your dreams for the future is a blessing in and of itself. You are in an enviable, highly favored place to have a spouse by your side for the long haul. Often, young couples are so busy with the daily hustle with family, jobs, etc., that discussions about longevity of marriage and living arrangements slip through the cracks. Have you decided as a couple where you want to live after retirement? Some couples like the simple life that rural living provides while others enjoy the conveniences of city life. Perhaps you want to purchase a vacation home near the ocean or in the mountains. Some of these thoughts may have already been revealed and discussed in the list of desires from the exercise you completed. Just keep in mind that it is never too early to begin planning your future together.

Also, consider the role of your spouse in your own personal short and long term goals. Have you shared with your spouse the things you have not yet accomplished or experienced? Maybe it is attending the super bowl game, mastering golf, traveling abroad, learning to swim, or starting a prison ministry. Your mate may be very helpful in helping to make your dream(s) come true.

As you plan your future together, do not neglect to discuss your final wishes. Perhaps you want to have a will prepared to reduce the clarify legal and financial issues for your spouse and family. If you desire to have a living will or if you want to be an organ donor, you should share that information with your spouse also.

God is pleased that you have chosen to honor your commitment to your marriage. Do not settle for a mediocre union because marriage is blessed by God. With God on your side, expect and work toward an exceptional marriage. Enjoy today, and always remember to plan for your tomorrow so as you age, you will enjoy the memories that you have created along your journey together.

UNTIL DEATH DO US PART COMMITMENT STATEMENT

I commit to do _____
and _____
to honor my lifetime commitment to God and my spouse.

_____   _____

Signed by   Date

_____   _____

Witnessed and signed by spouse   Date

Don't forget to document the day that this commitment pledge was fulfilled to your spouse's satisfaction.

On _____, my spouse has fulfilled his/her commitment and promise.

_____   _____

Signed by   Date

_____   _____

Acknowledged and signed by spouse Date

His & Her closing prayer

(Recite together)

Lord, teach us to number our days. We thank you for your protection from all hurt, harm, and danger. It is our desire to please you. From this day forward, we will not let the sun set when we are angry with one another. We will honor our commitment to remain married *until death us do part*. We ask you to continue to bless our marriage so we may be an example to others of what a marriage looks like when you are put first. We will gladly continue to give you all the praise, glory, and honor. In Jesus' name, we pray. Amen.

✿ Chapter 9 ✿

Conclusion

The Other Side Of Endurance is a place that brings joy, satisfaction and contentment. You and your spouse can enjoy all the benefits of a healthy and thriving marriage when you reach this milestone. Our goal with this workbook has been to design a tool to help you better understand your vows and the biblical principles of marriage. Progress begins with action. You have already taken important steps toward self-evaluation and begun to acknowledge your unique role in strengthening your marriage by completing the commitment pledges in this workbook. These pages will serve as a written record for you and your spouse to track your progress together. Your spouse does not expect you to be perfect, but he/she does expect you to strive to be the best you can be, and the commitment pledges will serve as a great aid in helping you fulfill that goal. Ideally, your spouse will also complete the exercises and pledges. In any event, press forward and apply the principles we have shared with you in this text, and you will be blessed. With prayer and faith in God, even the most troubling situations can be corrected.

Be encouraged. God wants you to prosper in all areas of your life. While negative messages from the world, friends, or family might suggest marital bliss is unachievable, or more specifically, that your marriage is doomed, you can reject the prospect of failure by placing Christ at the center of your life. Many mountaintop experiences require you to first go through the valley, so you should maintain realistic expectations in your

Conclusion

marriage. With this workbook, you now have tools to help you make it through your challenging times with greater ease.

The Other Side Of Endurance is a place in marriage where you 'know' you are together because of God's goodness. No other explanation sums it up better. *The Other Side Of Endurance* is a peaceful and precious destination where issues are handled harmoniously. The journey to this milestone can be rough and rocky. Our prayer is that you will realize that you can make it. Utilize the scriptures, prayers, and exercises in this book, and enjoy your journey together. Learn from your mistakes and value each victory as a stepping stone to an everlasting marriage. We pray that your commitment deepens and your bond of love is strengthened. Celebrate each other and allow nothing or no one to stand between your marriage vows to God, your spouse, and yourself.

We want your marriage to be strong in commitment, caring for each other in your communication, and joyous in your love making. And most of all, we want you to grow stronger together and experience the power of being grounded in the Word of God.

TO GOD BE THE GLORY FOR THE THINGS HE HAS DONE!!